Cell Communication

Understanding How Information Is Stored and Used in Cells

Michael Friedman and Brett Friedman

The Rosen Publishing Group, Inc., New York

For Gloria and Wynn Friedman

Published in 2005 by The Rosen Publishing Group, Inc.
29 East 21st Street, New York, NY 10010

First Edition

Library of Congress Cataloging-in-Publication

Friedman, Michael, 1955–
Cell communication: understanding how information is stored and used in cells/by Michael Friedman and Brett Friedman.
    p. cm.—(The library of cells)
Includes bibliographical references and index.
ISBN 1-4042-0319-2 (lib. bdg.)
1. Cell interaction—Juvenile literature.
I. Friedman, Brett. II. Title. III. Series.
QH604.2.F75 2005
571.6—dc22

                                        2004017048

Manufactured in the United States of America

On the cover: This is a colored electron transmission micrograph of DNA and messenger RNA (mRNA) molecules during the process of transcription, when genetic information from DNA is copied to mRNA. Transcription is the first step of protein synthesis.

Contents

Introduction

More than 150 years ago, scientists discovered that all living things are made up of cells. This includes every living animal and plant. In fact, every one of us has about 100 trillion cells in his or her body.

A cell is the smallest unit of matter capable of performing the processes of life. This means that an individual cell can carry out the same activities as a human body. However, each cell carries them out on a much smaller scale. For instance, cells can take in nutrients and turn them into energy for their various activities. Cells can respond to the conditions around them. Cells can also make copies of themselves capable of living on after the "parent" cell is dead.

The cells that make up a single living creature all have certain features in common. Each of them has a cell membrane that separates the cell from its environment. Each cell also has a set of organelles, which are like tiny organs that do the work of keeping the cell alive. For instance, the organelles that act as the cell's "furnace," where food is turned into energy, are called mitochondria. (The singular form of the word is "mitochondrion.")

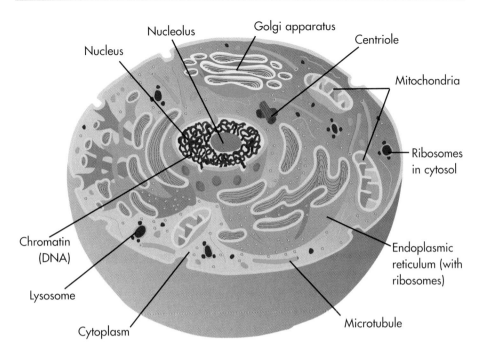

Nucleus
Nucleolus
Golgi apparatus
Centriole
Mitochondria
Ribosomes in cytosol
Chromatin (DNA)
Endoplasmic reticulum (with ribosomes)
Lysosome
Cytoplasm
Microtubule

The organelles of a eukaryotic cell are illustrated in this diagram. The cell's nucleus stores DNA material in the form of chromosomes and chromatin. Proteins created in the endoplasmic reticulum are then modified and stored in the Golgi apparatus. Mitochondria are responsible for cellular respiration. Microtubules and centrioles, located throughout the jellylike cytoplasm, help the cell keep its shape. Lysosomes contain digestive enzymes.

The cell also creates the proteins it needs to repair itself and create new cells in an organelle called the endoplasmic reticulum. The organelle called the Golgi apparatus then packages those proteins and exports them to the cell.

All the cells in a living creature carry the same hereditary material called deoxyribonucleic acid, or DNA. DNA is stored in the cell nucleus. It is the "blueprint" for the manufacture of all new cells. When a body grows or repairs an injury, it follows the blueprint in the DNA. That is why a body's new cells can live alongside and work with the old ones— because they all follow the same set of instructions.

Although all the cells in the human body share the same DNA, they are not exactly alike. Cells need to be different from one another so they can carry out specific jobs. Some cells transport oxygen and nutrients and help the body respond to sickness and injury. These are called blood cells. Bone cells make up the skeleton that enables the body to stand erect. Still other cells make it possible for the body to process information about the world around it. These are called nerve cells, or neurons.

But to do all the jobs the body needs, all of its cells must work together. In some cases, this means working with other cells of the same type. In other cases, it means working with cells of different types. In both situations, cells must communicate effectively with each other.

Chapter One

Communication Within the Cell

DNA looks like two connected strands in a spiral. You may want to think of it as a twisted ladder. Each part of the ladder is organized in a specific way. DNA doesn't just provide instructions for the construction of new cells. It also directs the activities of the organelles in our cells. It tells them which structures to make and what to do with them. This is critical to the cell's continued health and survival.

Although the DNA found in a cell's nucleus contains instructions for every organelle, the DNA itself never leaves the nucleus. It is like a precious document that must be kept in a bank vault. However, the contents of such a document can still be read if copies of it are made and distributed.

DNA instructions can be copied, too, through a process called transcription. It is in this way that genetic information within the original DNA can be transferred without the DNA ever leaving the safety of the cell's nucleus. This process requires the presence in the nucleus of nucleotides and an enzyme called RNA polymerase. Nucleotides are the chemical compounds that serve as the building

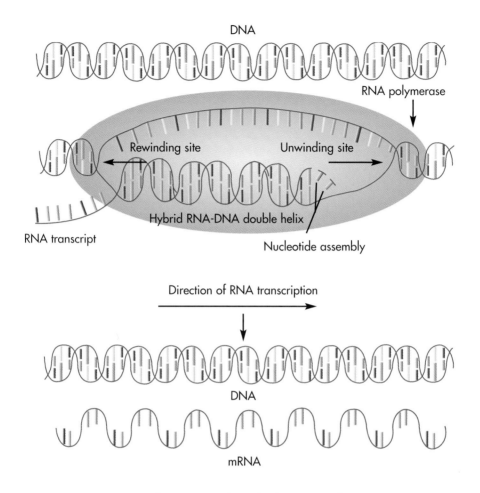

DNA

RNA polymerase

Rewinding site

Unwinding site

Hybrid RNA-DNA double helix

RNA transcript

Nucleotide assembly

Direction of RNA transcription

DNA

mRNA

During transcription (the process by which DNA information is copied into RNA creating messenger RNA, or mRNA), genetic information flows from DNA to RNA. The same genetic information in mRNA is then used, with the help of RNA polymerase, to create proteins in a separate process called translation. These interdependencies occur in all living cells.

blocks for DNA. An enzyme is a protein that makes possible or increases the rate of a chemical reaction.

When RNA polymerase is present in the nucleus, it creates links between free-floating nucleotides. They are bound to and arranged in the same order as the DNA. The new molecule that is created through this process is called RNA, or ribonucleic acid.

RNA looks like only one twisted strand, not two. That is because it isn't involved in the construction of new cells. RNA only carries instructions to the organelles, so it doesn't need two strands of information to do its job.

Biologists have discovered that there are actually three kinds of RNA, each one made possible by a different RNA polymerase. Messenger RNA (mRNA), is the kind that carries the coded instructions that originate in DNA, such as which kinds of proteins will be produced outside the nucleus.

However, mRNA cannot make proteins by itself. All it can do is give instructions. Messenger RNA needs a partner to do the work. That partner is called a ribosome.

The Journey of the Ribosome

A ribosome is a structure created in a specialized part of the nucleus called the nucleolus. Ribosomes are always composed of two subunits, each one comprising various proteins and a second kind of RNA called ribosomal RNA, or rRNA. One subunit is always bigger than the other.

When the subunits are created in the nucleolus, they are separate. Later, outside the nucleus, they bind together. But first, they have to emerge from the nucleus, which is enclosed in a protective membrane. This membrane keeps the nucleus separate from the cytoplasm, which is the jellylike substance that surrounds all of the organelles inside a cell.

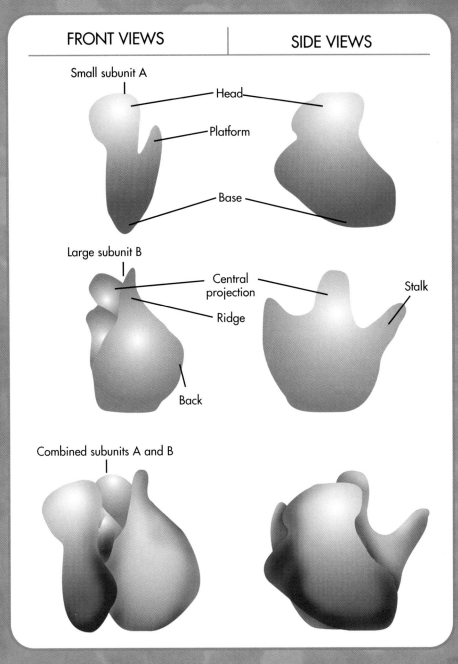

| FRONT VIEWS | SIDE VIEWS |

Small subunit A

Head

Platform

Base

Large subunit B

Central projection

Ridge

Stalk

Back

Combined subunits A and B

The front and side views of prokaryotic ribosomes, as well as their main parts, are pictured. Ribosomes, which are made up of RNA and proteins, are organelles composed of two subunits (top), the ribosome, and its attendant molecule. Ribosomes translate mRNA into proteins from a set of genetic instructions during translation. In the lower diagram, the large and small ribosome subunits A and B are united. Eukaryotic ribosomes share a similar structure.

Cellular Membranes

Cellular membranes are made up of two kinds of building blocks—proteins and lipids. Lipids are fatty compound molecules that, like proteins, are found in all living cells.

A cell features several kinds of membranes. One of them encloses the entire cell and keeps it separate from other cells in the body. This membrane is called the cell or plasma membrane. Each organelle within the cell also has individual membranes.

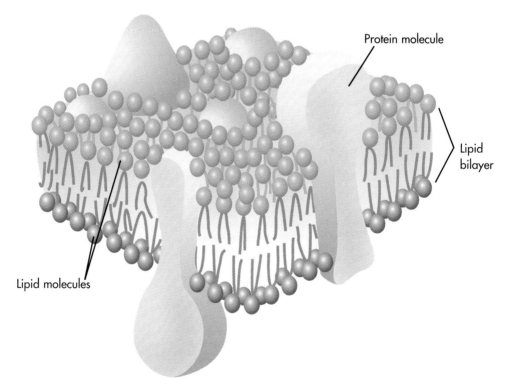

Many cell membranes are two-layer structures that utilize a lipid bilayer system, which is an arrangement of millions of lipid molecules. The lipid molecule "head" is hydrophilic ("water loving") and its tail is hydrophobic ("water hating"). This system allows materials to enter and exit the cell and helps form a protective barrier that controls the loss of substances the cell needs to survive.

While membranes keep most material out, they also let some material in. In other words, they are selectively permeable.

Material Exits the Nucleus

The membrane around the nucleus—also called the nuclear envelope—is actually a double membrane. That makes it more difficult for most matter to get in or out of the nucleus. However, the nuclear envelope also has pores, or holes, through which only proteins, ribosomal subunits, and RNA can pass. Each of these holes is about ten billionths of a meter in diameter, which is very small.

Because these pores are not big enough for a complete ribosome to pass through them, the ribosomal subunits must divide and join together afterward. The nuclear pores also permit two forms of RNA to leave the nucleus. One kind is mRNA, which we have already discussed. The other kind is transfer RNA, also known as tRNA.

The Endoplasmic Reticulum

When mRNA and the two ribosomal subunits leave the nucleus, some of them travel to an organelle that shares a membrane with the nucleus. This organelle, called the endoplasmic reticulum, is a collection of tubes. These tubes serve as a highway for the movement of material within the cell. The endoplasmic reticulum also provides a convenient setting for the creation of proteins.

The first step in the protein-making process is the combination of mRNA and the two ribosomal subunits. The mRNA helps bring the subunits together into a complete ribosome, which can manufacture protein molecules according to the code supplied by the DNA. But the ribosome cannot go to work until it gains the raw materials that are needed to create a protein. These raw materials are called amino acids.

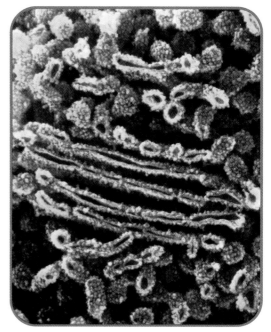

The endoplasmic reticulum (ER) in a human pancreatic cell has a network of folding membranes. This design allows maximum surface area for the ribosomes, seen here as small spheres, to synthesize proteins. The ER that has a granular appearance, as this one does, is referred to as the "rough" ER because of its ribosomes, while the "smooth" ER (not pictured) has no ribosomes and is concerned only with metabolizing fats.

Amino Acids

Amino acids are chemical compounds that float freely in a cell's cytoplasm. They are brought to the location of the ribosome by the transfer RNA. Only one kind of tRNA molecule is designed to attract a particular amino acid. The ability of a tRNA molecule to attract a specific amino acid is determined by its nucleotides.

Some Ribosomes Like to Wander

Not every ribosome winds up on the endoplasmic reticulum. Some move out into the cytoplasm. These ribosomes come together in clusters called polyribosomes. They are held together by a strand of mRNA. When amino acids are brought to polyribosomes, the mRNA strand can direct the assembly of proteins. The process is the same as when proteins are put together on the surface of the endoplasmic reticulum. After these proteins are manufactured, they are dispersed to different points in the cytoplasm.

We have all seen a key open a lock. What we don't usually see is the way the teeth of the key fit into the slots inside the lock. No other key will work in that lock because its teeth and the slots have to be perfectly aligned. This is the way nucleotides and amino acids fit together.

After the tRNA captures the amino acid, it guides it to the endoplasmic reticulum or to a free-floating cluster of ribosomes. There, the amino acid is introduced to a ribosome with mRNA that corresponds to that tRNA. But as we will see, the tRNA's job is still not over.

Translation

By this point in the process, the information encoded in the DNA molecule has helped create the two

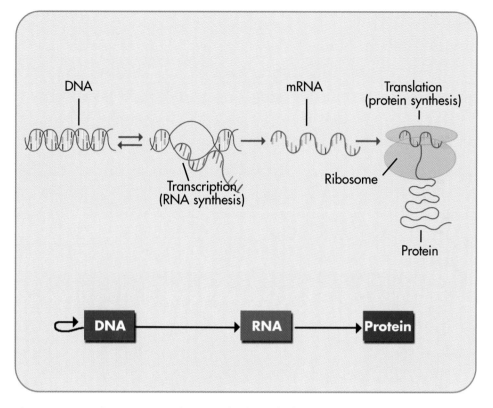

The process of protein synthesis, which includes both translation and transcription, is illustrated in this diagram. In transcription, genetic instructions are transferred to messenger RNA, or mRNA. In translation, mRNA travels to ribosomes located in the cell's cytoplasm. Transfer RNA, or tRNA, molecules work with mRNA to create proteins out of amino acids.

ribosomal subunits. They traveled through the nuclear envelope into the cytoplasm, tied the ribosomal subunits together, and attracted amino acids to the ribosome. However, to create a working protein, another process called translation must take place.

During translation, the ribosome, the tRNA, and the mRNA must work as a team. Together, they translate encoded information into a specific protein. The protein must be the one called for by the cell's DNA inside the nucleus.

Proteins are different from each other because of their amino acids. If the amino acids are strung in one order, they will make up one of the protein molecules in the cell membrane. If they are strung in another order, they will make up one of the protein molecules that leaves the cell to do work elsewhere in the body. And so on.

Two Kinds of Endoplasmic Reticulum

Only part of the endoplasmic reticulum in a cell allows ribosomes to collect on it and manufacture proteins. That portion is called the rough endoplasmic reticulum because, under a microscope, the ribosomes make its surface look rough. The other portion is called the smooth endoplasmic reticulum.

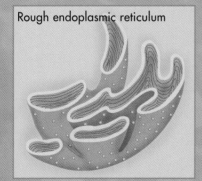

Rough endoplasmic reticulum

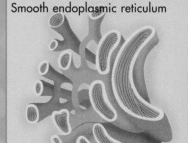

Smooth endoplasmic reticulum

The endoplasmic reticulum, or ER, is like an irregular maze. While the smooth ER manufactures mostly complex lipids (fats), the rough ER, studded with ribosomes, is among the main sites of protein manufacturing within a eukaryotic cell.

The ribosome cannot work directly with amino acids to ensure that they are strung in the correct order. However, it can work with the tRNA that is attached to the amino acids. The ribosome does this by matching up the tRNA to its mRNA, since they share complementary patterns of nucleotides.

In this way, the message originally contained in the DNA becomes a reality. A specific protein is created for use somewhere in the cell. But before it can do the job required of it, it must reach the part of the cell for which it was intended.

The Protein Highway

After a protein is made on the surface of the endoplasmic reticulum, it takes one of several routes. One possibility is that it will be drawn down into the membrane of the endoplasmic reticulum. In that case, it will become part of the organelle's phospholipid layer. Another possibility is that it will be dispatched to some other part of the cell, perhaps to aid in repair. A third possibility is that it will be passed on to the Golgi apparatus in small sacs called vesicles.

The Golgi apparatus is an organelle that shares a membrane with the endoplasmic reticulum. It is made up of Golgi bodies, which look like flattened balloons. The purpose of the Golgi apparatus is to package proteins and other molecules for export from the cell. In the next few chapters, we will see what happens to some of these exported proteins.

Chapter Two

Hormonal Communication

You can see that communication is important in your own community. Without proper communication, no one would know when schools were opened or closed, or when and where town meetings were taking place. And every fire engine, police car, and ambulance in town might respond to the same emergency, leaving no one available if other people required assistance.

The only way for a community to make efficient use of its resources is for everyone to effectively communicate. It works the same way in the human body. Cells must "talk" with other cells in order to perform the functions necessary for survival.

In a community, there is more than one way for people to talk with each other. They may meet on the street and speak face to face. They may talk on their telephones, either over long or short distances. Cells have developed various methods of communicating as well. This communication between cells is called cell signaling. Cells have developed four different types of cell communication: hormonal or endocrinal, paracrinal, autocrinal, and neuronal. The most common method is endocrinal, through the release of hormones.

Hormones Carry Instructions

A hormone is a chemical created by a group of cells in one part of the body that encourages activity in another part of the body. In other words, it carries a message that tells a second group of cells to do something.

Not all cells release hormones. Those that do are found in structures called glands. When we speak of all the glands in the body, we collectively refer to them as the endocrine system. Glands release hormones only under certain circumstances. They may be

Endocrinal Signaling

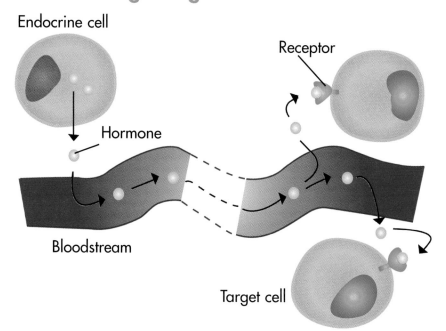

Endocrine cell

Receptor

Hormone

Bloodstream

Target cell

This diagram illustrates the process of communication between cells known as endocrinal signaling. Hormones produced in endocrine cells are released into the bloodstream and are distributed to target cells throughout the body. The release of hormones is the best method for sending messages between cells over long distances.

prompted to release a hormone as a reaction to something that is taking place outside the body. Or glands may release a hormone because of something that is taking place inside the body.

For the hormone to reach its target, it needs to travel in a bodily fluid. The most common example of such a fluid is the bloodstream. Sometimes the hormone's target is very close to the gland where the hormone is produced. In other instances, it may be far away.

Once the hormonal message gets into the bloodstream, it is able to reach cells in many different parts of the body. However, not every part is capable of responding to the hormonal message. Even when several types of cells can respond to it, only one type can respond in the desired manner.

Going back to our imaginary community, you can say to everyone at once, "Drive your vehicle to my house on Main Street and pick up the trash." However, not every vehicle in town is equipped to collect trash. In addition to sanitation vehicles, such a message might bring sports cars, ice-cream trucks, and even tricycles.

In a community, those who send messages only want a response from a particular person or group of people. In this example, they want to reach the person who drives the sanitation vehicle. Only he or she is equipped to do the job in question.

In the same way, cells that send out hormonal information want a response from a specific kind of cell. The body ensures that this will happen with a cell's surface receptors. A surface receptor is a structure on the outside of a cell that marks it as the target for a particular hormonal message. When the hormone reaches that cell, it recognizes the receptor and delivers its information.

Helpers on the Inside

In many cases, hormones are released in small amounts and act slowly on their target cells. Rather than ask for an immediate effect, hormones produce changes slowly over time. However, hormones do not actually enter a cell to achieve this change. They are too large to pass through the cell's outer membrane.

The cell membrane is composed of two layers. Each one contains lipids, which are fatty substances present in every cell. For this reason, it is described as a lipid bilayer (the prefix "bi" meaning "two"). The cell membrane also contains proteins, which are complex molecules made up of smaller molecules called amino acids. The proteins give the membrane its toughness and the lipids give it flexibility.

Although some molecules are small enough to enter the molecule directly, this is not the case with hormones. How, then, can they get their message to the necessary organelle in the target cell? Hormones depend on the cell's surface receptors to pass the message along. In order to do this, surface receptors have to reach down through the membrane. Think of a tree. It has branches with leaves that we can see easily enough. However, it also has roots that reach down deep into the soil. That is how a surface receptor is positioned—both above the outer membrane of the cell and below it.

Once the surface receptor passes the message through the lipid bilayer into the cell, another kind of message-carrying molecule takes over. This is called a second messenger. It is a protein designed to take the message from the surface receptor to its final destination inside the cell. Only after the message is delivered inside the target cell can that cell do the job required of it.

The Fight-or-Flight Hormone

Let's look at a real-world example of how a hormonal message can produce a cellular response. Imagine yourself threatened by a bully on the way to school. You may decide to stand your ground and defend yourself. On the other hand, you may decide it is smarter to run away. Either way, you will need a great deal of energy to accomplish your task.

After your brain processes the threat, it prompts the cells in your adrenal glands to release a hormone. This hormone is called epinephrine. It travels through your bloodstream until it comes to a particular surface receptor that is only located on muscle cells. The surface receptor then passes on the hormonal message to a second messenger inside the cell. It is this second messenger that asks the muscle cell to do a particular job.

In this case, the job is to break down the carbohydrates stored in your muscles into energy. That energy can then be used in muscle contraction. Your muscles will then enable you to either defend yourself against our imaginary bully or run away as quickly as you can.

This is a light micrograph of crystals of the hormone epinephrine, more commonly known as adrenaline. Produced in the adrenal glands above the kidneys, adrenaline is released into the bloodstream during moments of great stress, fear, and emotion. Adrenaline helps prepare the body during stressful moments by widening the airways of lungs, constricting small blood vessels, and allowing the body to utilize its store of sugar for a quick burst of energy.

Of course, a number of things can go wrong with this system. A surface receptor on a particular muscle cell may not pass the hormonal message on to a second messenger. A second messenger may not do a good job of giving the message to the organelles inside the cell. In either case, the muscle cell will not break down its stored carbohydrates into energy.

Fortunately, the body has a backup system. Each cell in our bodies has a set of gap junctions on its surface. Gap junctions are protein structures that permit the passage of small molecules through holes in the cell membranes. Those small molecules can then pass from one cell to another.

Second messenger molecules are small enough to pass through a cell's gap junctions. In doing so, they can travel from their original cell to its neighboring cells. In this case, even if a cell's own second messenger doesn't do the job, its neighbor's second messenger can do it. The cell will still produce the required response.

When Hormones Get Out of Line

Sometimes, getting the hormonal message to the target cell is not the problem. In some cases, the target cell receives the message when it shouldn't. In this scenario, the target cell works when it should be at rest. This creates health problems for the human body.

One example of this is the hormonal disorder called acromegaly. Acromegaly typically affects middle-aged adults. It gets its name from the Greek words *acro* or "extremity" and *megaly* or "enlargement." One of its most common symptoms is the abnormal growth of the hands and feet.

Under normal circumstances, a person grows only during childhood and adolescence. This process starts when a part of the brain called the hypothalamus creates a growth hormone–releasing hormone, or GHRH. GHRH is sent through the bloodstream to the pituitary gland, which is located at the base of the brain. GHRH's message to the pituitary gland is to make a second hormone called growth hormone, or GH. After GH is introduced to the bloodstream, it reaches the liver. The liver then produces a third hormone called insulin-like growth factor, or IGF-1.

It is the IGF-1 that causes the growth of bones and other parts of the body. This continues until the child reaches adulthood. At that point, IGF-1 normally signals the pituitary gland to cut off GH production. Sometimes, however, the pituitary gland continues to make GH. It is this continued production of GH that results in abnormal growth, or in this case, acromegaly.

The first sign that someone is afflicted with acromegaly is usually a change in ring or shoe size. As the disease gets worse, facial bones are affected. The brow and lower jaw start to stick out, the nose gets bigger, and the teeth grow farther apart. Other symptoms are weakness, headaches, and the enlargement of organs such as the liver, kidneys, and heart.

Perhaps the most famous case of acromegaly is that of the wrestler Andre the Giant. Because his body produced too much GH, he was nearly 7 feet tall (2.1 meters) by the time he was seventeen years old. As an adult, he was 7 feet 4 inches (2.2 m) tall. Considering his height, one would expect his hands and feet to be larger than those of an ordinary man. His feet were 23 inches (58 centimeters) long. That is much larger than an average man's foot.

When Andre the Giant reached his forties, his health began to suffer. His enlarged organs stopped doing their jobs. In his final years, he was in a great deal of pain. Finally, acromegaly claimed his life when he was forty-six years old.

Acromegaly is typically treated with drugs, radiation therapy, and sometimes surgery. The goal is to restore normal function to the pituitary gland. If this is accomplished, some of the disease's effects may be reversed. Others, unfortunately, are permanent.

Communication: Local Possibilities

Hormones play an important role in cell-to-cell communication. They enable cells in one part of the body to give instructions to cells in a distant part of the body. However, hormones tend to act slowly over time. Cells close to each other sometimes need other ways to send information.

When cells are the same, as in the case of muscle cells or bone cells, they are touching one another membrane to membrane. Such cells can send small molecules (such as second messengers) back and forth, admitting them through the gap junctions in each cell's membrane.

Even when cells are not touching, they can send messages to neighboring cells in the form of mole-cules. The receptors on the receiving cells will then bind the molecules together and take them in. These messages are known as paracrine signals. Paracrine

Contact-dependent Signaling

Signaling cell   Target cell

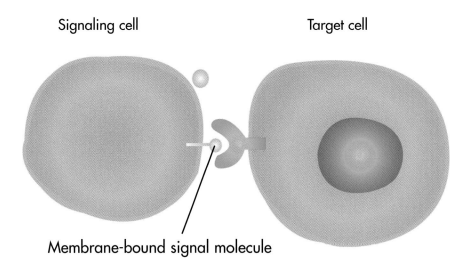

Membrane-bound signal molecule

Only cells that have direct membrane-to-membrane contact with one another can communicate by the contact-dependent method. Even though a cell might still communicate by the release of a similar signal molecule during this process, the information is sent much faster and more efficiently by membrane-to-membrane contact.

signals are used when cells in a particular part of the body need to act in a coordinated way.

In some cases, a signal may act on the cell that produced it. When that happens, it is called an autocrine signal.

Chapter Three

Neuronal Communication

As we have seen, the human body has several ways to put its cells to work. We have learned, for instance, that paracrine signals act more quickly than hormonal (or endocrinal) signals do. However, some cells need an even faster system to carry out the tasks assigned to them.

These cells are called nerve cells, or neurons. They are the cells found in the body's nervous system. The nervous system includes the brain, the spine, and the nerves that are distributed throughout the body. Neurons use special kinds of amino acids called neurotransmitters to send information from one neuron to another.

Signals transferred by neurotransmitters travel very rapidly. Sometimes they move more than 250 miles per hour (402 kilometers per hour)—as fast as a jumbo passenger jet. However, neurotransmitters only work over very short distances. In this way they are different from hormones, which may have to travel from one end of the body to the other.

Neurotransmitters are also different from hormones in that they may be released on a conscious

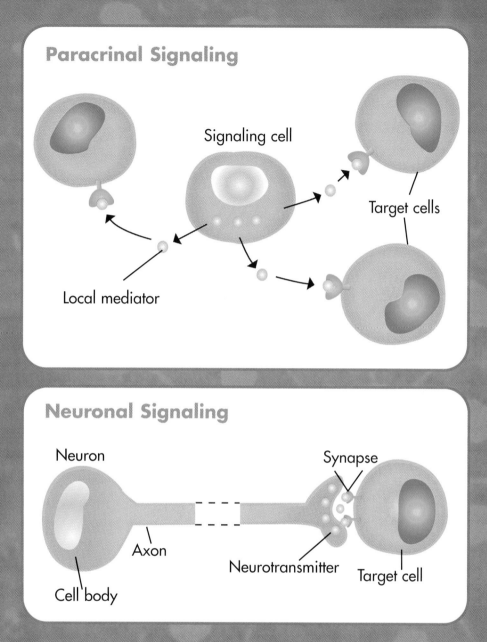

Paracrinal Signaling

Signaling cell

Target cells

Local mediator

Neuronal Signaling

Neuron

Synapse

Axon

Neurotransmitter

Target cell

Cell body

Unlike in endocrinal signaling, where hormones carry a cell's message over a long distance, paracrine signaling *(top)* is done over short distances to neighboring cells. This is a common method employed by cells at sites of inflammation and infection. Neuronal signals *(bottom)* travel along enclosed axons very quickly (up to 328 feet per second [100 meters per second]) and effectively. At the point of contact, that same signal is transferred to a chemical signal called a neurotransmitter. The tiny gap where this exchange takes place is called the synapse.

basis. For instance, when a person makes an effort to remember something, neurotransmitters are sent from neuron to neuron in the brain. Hormones, on the other hand, are automatically released. We cannot send them out at will.

Anatomy of a Neuron

The average human brain is composed of about 100 billion neurons. Obviously, these are very small, though they do vary in shape and size. In many ways, neurons are similar to other cells in the body. For instance, they are surrounded by a cell membrane. They contain a nucleus, mitochondria, an endoplasmic reticulum, and other organelles. However, neurons also differ from other cells in the body.

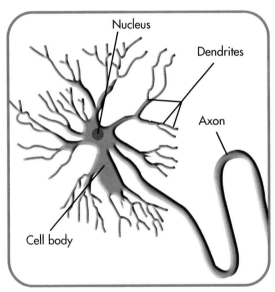

Nucleus

Dendrites

Axon

Cell body

This illustration shows the basic parts of a typical nerve cell, or neuron. While the neuron's axon acts as an electrical "conductor," sending information between cells, the dendrites receive that information. As in other cells, the nucleus acts as the neuron's control center. The human brain contains about a hundred billion neurons, each of them working together to process information.

Unlike other cells, neurons have special parts that stick out from the main body of the cell. These are called dendrites and axons. Dendrites have a rough surface and carry information to the neuron. Axons have a smooth surface and carry information away from the neuron. Generally, a neuron will have only one axon but many dendrites.

Another difference between neurons and other cells lies in the neurons' inability to reproduce. Though other cells in the body die and are replaced, most neurons are not replaced when they die. This means that a person is born with all the neurons he or she is ever likely to have. Recently, scientists theorized that there is only one part of the brain, the hippocampus, where new neurons may be created.

Bridging the Gap

In order to communicate with each other, neurons form a special connection called a synapse. The synapse is the gap the neurotransmitter must cross when it carries information from neuron to neuron. It consists of three parts.

The first part of the synapse is called the presynaptic ending. This is the part of the neuron that sends messages, the same part that contains neurotransmitters. It may be an axon, a dendrite, or a section of the neuron's main body.

The second part of the synapse is the postsynaptic ending. This is the part of the receiving neuron that contains special receptors. These receptors act as targets for the neurotransmitters.

The third part of the synapse is the synaptic cleft, which is the gap between the presynaptic ending and the postsynaptic ending. It is this space that the neurotransmitter must cross in order to reach the receiving neuron.

However, neurotransmitters do not normally cross the synaptic cleft independently. They need a push in the form of an electrical impulse. This electrical impulse is generated within the message-sending neuron. One impulse is enough to send a number of transmitters shooting across the synaptic cleft.

As the neurotransmitters move into the space between the neurons, they spread out. This enables them to reach more than one of the receptors located on the postsynaptic ending. This is important because it will take more than one neurotransmitter to get the desired response.

When a neurotransmitter reaches a receptor, it creates a change in the receiving neuron. It makes that neuron more likely to follow the directions contained in the neurotransmitter. If enough neurotransmitters reach the receiving neuron with the same message, it will create what scientists call an action potential. The action the neuron takes will be to send out an electrical impulse of its own. In this way, it passes on the message contained in the neurotransmitters.

The Need for Accuracy

Communication in the nervous system is not just faster than other kinds of cellular communication within the body; it's also much more precise. There is no chance of the wrong neuron getting the information.

But then, if you wanted to get important information to a specific person, you wouldn't broadcast it

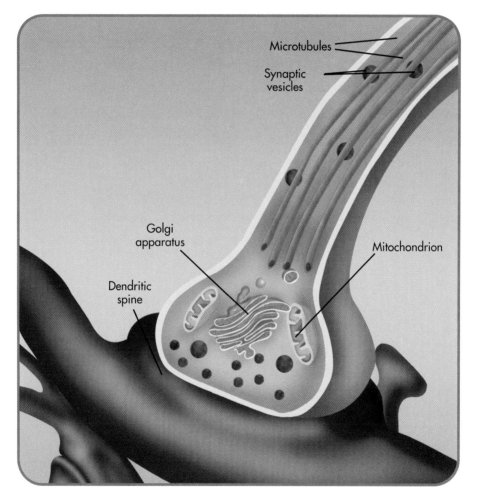

Microtubules

Synaptic vesicles

Golgi apparatus

Mitochondrion

Dendritic spine

This diagram of a neuron shows some of its organelles. Neurons connect with other neurons through synapses, which is the exact point where the electric or chemical information is transferred. In the case of chemical transmission, neurotransmitters molecules are released through the presynaptic membrane to a microscopic space called the synaptic cleft and then to the postsynaptic membrane. This entire process takes 0.5 to 0.4 milliseconds.

on the public channels of radio or television. You would call the person on the telephone and speak privately to him or her. In the same way, neurons do not depend on the "public" bloodstream to carry their messages. They have their own private channel: the synapse.

Also, neurons do not pass on a message after they receive a single neurotransmitter. They wait until they have received enough of them to create an action potential. Then they send out an electrical impulse that allows the message to move to the next neuron in line. This communication between neurons needs to be controlled and efficient because the ability to make quick decisions is necessary for survival.

Chapter Four

When Things Go Wrong

Thanks to our highly developed nervous systems and all the quick-acting neurons in them, we have survived as a species. Unfortunately, we sometimes encounter substances that prevent our nervous systems from acting quickly—or at all.

One such substance is called a neurotoxin. A neurotoxin is what we commonly think of as a poison. It may come from a spider, a snake, a scorpion, a bee, a fish, or even a plant. These living things use neurotoxins to protect themselves against predators, including human beings, or to capture their prey.

A neurotoxin works by blocking cell communication in the nervous system. More specifically, it prevents certain neurotransmitters from crossing the synaptic cleft. When that happens, the body is prevented from taking certain actions. If the action in question is feeling one's fingertips, the neurotoxin may prove an inconvenience. If the action is something as critical as breathing, the neurotoxin may prove fatal.

Some natural secretions, like those from this poison arrow frog *(left)*, possess toxins that are harmful to humans. Alkaloid-producing poison glands positioned across the frog's body can affect the human nervous system when they are absorbed through the skin's layers. The liver and ovaries of this puffer fish *(right)* contain a poison deadly to humans called tetrodotoxin. Although eating puffer fish can be fatal, they are considered a delicacy in Japan.

Opiates and Neurotransmitters

Psychoactive drugs are other substances that can affect the efficiency of the nervous system. In some cases, psychoactive drugs affect the release of neurotransmitters in the brain. In other cases, they affect the availability of receptor locations on the postsynaptic ending.

Opium is an example of a psychoactive drug. It is found in the opium poppy, a plant that grows wild in the Middle East, Southeast Asia, Central America, and South America. Drugs that come from opium are called opiates. They reduce pain and discomfort and produce a pleasurable sensation throughout the body. Opiates are administered to people after surgical procedures and are sometimes given as prescriptions to people who suffer from chronic pain.

The main ingredient in opium is morphine. Doctors used morphine freely during the American Civil War (1861–1865) to ease the pain of wounded soldiers.

The milky inside of this unripe opium seed carpel (capsule) is seeping out after the carpel has been cut. Once the substance hardens after it has been exposed to air, it is scraped off and formed into balls containing the natural pain-relieving substances used to make morphine, heroin, and codeine. The scientific name for the opium poppy is *Papaver somniferum.*

After the war, doctors continued to prescribe medicines with morphine in them.

Unfortunately, physicians working in the 1800s didn't fully understand the opiates they prescribed. The drugs often caused more misery than the pain they treated. Patients eventually became addicted to morphine. An addiction is an unhealthy dependence on a drug. Usually an individual is so driven to take the drug that his or her health is compromised.

Scientists tried to address this situation by coming up with a treatment safer than morphine. In 1874, they produced a new drug called heroin. Heroin comes from morphine and has similar effects, but was supposed to be less addictive. The Bayer company manufactured heroin in 1898. It was intended to take morphine's place in drugstores as a pain reliever. It was also said to cure persistent coughs.

Heroin did reduce pain. It also gave people a drowsy sense of well-being and reduced people's tendency to cough. However, it also had a number of

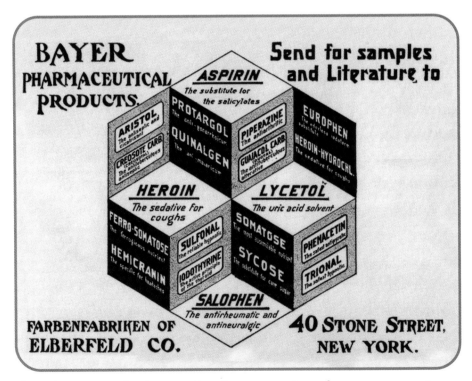

This advertisement for Bayer pain relievers contains references to narcotics such as heroin. In 1900, when this magazine ad originally appeared, narcotics such as heroin were commonly administered to the public by local pharmacists. The Bayer company originally introduced heroin in 1898 as a cough suppressant that did not have the harmful effects of other opiates.

negative effects. People who took heroin became nauseous, lost body heat, and had trouble breathing.

Even worse, heroin turned out to be just as addictive as morphine. Several hours after a person took the drug, he or she wanted more of it. If the person didn't get more heroin, he or she experienced physical symptoms of withdrawal that included fever, body cramps, and chills. In addition, the longer a person took the drug, the more of it he or she needed to obtain the same pleasurable effect. By 1924, the U.S. government recognized the harmful effects of heroin. It passed a law against its sale and possession. Heroin has been an illegal drug in the United States ever since.

Why do drugs like heroin and morphine reduce pain and produce a pleasurable sensation? Scientists tried to figure that out for a long time. Finally, in 1973, they made a discovery that began to offer an explanation. They found that some of the neurons in the human nervous system had receptors that accepted opiates. These receptors were located in the parts of the brain used for breathing, feeling pain, and experiencing emotions.

Scientists wondered why neurons would have receptors so perfectly suited to opiates. What purpose did these receptors serve? In 1975, they came up with an answer. They discovered that the brain manufactures certain neurotransmitters that act like opiates. These neurotransmitters, called endorphins, reduce pain and produce a feeling of well-being. Endorphins are always present in the brain. However, they are released in greater amounts when people are in pain or experiencing stress.

Heroin addiction is difficult to treat. However, doctors have had success with drugs developed for just this purpose. One of these drugs is naloxone. Naloxone molecules bind themselves to opiate receptors so opiates cannot work as they normally would. Another drug used to fight heroin addiction is methadone. Methadone also blocks opiates from reaching their receptors.

Conclusion

As we have seen, effective means of communication are essential to the smooth working of the human body. This is true at the level of the individual cell, where DNA messages are responsible for the production of various proteins. It is also true of the messages that pass from cell to cell. These messages may occur as the result of endocrinal activity, paracrinal activity, cell-to-cell contact, or the production of neurotransmitters that carry information through the nervous system.

We have discussed these various methods of communication as if they act in isolation from each other. In reality, they are all part of a single complex system. Messages carried by hormones trigger messages in the brain. Messages in the brain trigger paracrine messages sent from one muscle cell to another. Every process is designed to work together.

When any of these message systems is prevented from doing its job, the entire human body suffers. This is true whether the failure is the result of natural causes, as in the case of acromegaly, or the use of habit-forming drugs like heroin. In some cases, these failures may even lead to death.

However, when hormones and neurotransmitters pass information along smoothly and efficiently, the body works like a finely tuned machine. It is the continuing goal of medical science to better understand and prevent what can go wrong with the body's communication systems, ensuring better lives for all of us.

Glossary

amino acids (uh-MEE-noh A-sidz) Molecules that serve as the building blocks of proteins.

axon (AK-son) Long, thin nerve fibers capable of rapidly conducting nerve impulses over long distances to deliver signals to other cells.

cell (SEL) The basic unit of life.

cell signaling (SEL SIG-nuh-ling) Communication between cells by extracellular chemical signals.

cytoplasm (SY-toh-plah-zum) The jellylike interior of a cell.

dendrite (DEN-dryt) The branched extension of a nerve cell that receives stimuli from other nerve cells.

deoxyribonucleic acid (dee-OK-see-ri-boh-noo-klay-ik A-sid) Also called DNA. The molecules of genes; the chemical basis of hereditary traits.

endocrine system (EN-doh-krin SIS-tum) The collection of glands that makes and sends out hormones.

endoplasmic reticulum (en-do-PLAHS-mik reh-TIH-kyoo-lum) A membrane-bound compartment in the cytoplasm of eukaryotic cells, where lipids are secreted and membrane-bound proteins are made.

endorphins (en-DOR-finz) Neurotransmitters that reduce pain and produce a feeling of well-being.

Golgi apparatus (GOHL-jee ah-pehr-AH-tus) The organelle in the cell that packages proteins for export from the cell.

hormone (HOR-mohn) A chemical in your body that controls the activities of certain organs and tissues.

hypothalamus (hy-poh-THA-luh-mus) The part of the brain that controls emotions.

mitochondria (my-toh-KON-dree-ah) The organelles in the cell that produce energy by combining nutrients with oxygen.

neuron (NUR-on) Cells that carry messages from the brain to other parts in the body.

neurotoxins (NUR-oh-tok-sinz) Poisonous substances that attack the nerves and nerve tissues.

neurotransmitter (nur-oh-TRANS-mih-ter) A molecule that passes information from one neuron to another.

nucleus (NOO-klee-us) A rounded structure inside the cell that acts as the cell's control center.

organelle (OR-gah-nel) Structures found in the cytoplasm of a cell that perform the same types of jobs as organs do in the human body.

ribonucleic acid (ry-boh-noo-KLAY-ik A-sid) Also called RNA. A chemical that carries hereditary information and is involved with manufacturing proteins.

ribosome (RY-bo-zohm) The structures in the cytoplasm of a cell that manufacture proteins.

synapse (SIH-naps) The gap between neurons that must be crossed by a neurotransmitter.

translation (tranz-LAY-shun) The process by which ribosomes string together amino acids to make proteins.

transcription (tran-SKRIP-shun) The process by which genetic information is shared and messenger RNA is created from a template of a DNA molecule.

For More Information

Discover Magazine
114 Fifth Avenue
New York, NY 10011
(212) 633-4400
Web site: http://www.discover.com

National Institutes of Health
9000 Rockville Pike
Bethesda, MD 20892
(301) 496-4000
e-mail: NIHinfo@od.nih.gov
Web site: http://www.nih.gov

National Science Foundation
4201 Wilson Boulevard
Arlington, VA 22230
(703) 292-5111
Web site: http://www.nsf.gov

Web Sites

Due to the changing nature of Internet links, the Rosen Publishing Group, Inc., has developed an online list of Web sites related to the subject of this book. This site is updated regularly. Please use this link to access the list:

http://www.rosenlinks.com/lce/ceco

For Further Reading

Fichter, George S. *Cells: A First Book*. London, England: Franklin Watts, 1986.

Parker, Steve. *Eyewitness: Human Body* (Eyewitness Books). New York: DK Publishing, 2003.

Silverstein, Alvin, Virginia Silverstein, and Laura Silverstein Nunn. *Cells*. Brookfield, CT: Twenty-first Century Books, 2002.

Van Cleave, Janice Pratt. *Biology for Every Kid*. New York: John Wiley & Sons, Inc., 1995.

Wallace, Holly. *Cells and Systems*. Chicago, IL: Heinemann Library, 2000.

Bibliography

Alberts, Bray, Johnson, Lewis, Raff, Roberts, Walter.
   Forms of Cell Signaling. Oxfordshire, England:
   Garland Publishing, 1998.

Berger, Melvin. *Enzymes in Action*. New York: Thomas Y.
   Crowell Company, 1971.

Dalbecco, Renato. *The Design of Life*. New Haven, CT:
   Yale University Press, 1995.

Gliese, Arthur C. *Cell Physiology*. Austin, TX: Saunders
   College Publishing-Holt, Rhinehart & Winston, 1973.

Index

About the Authors

Michael Friedman is the author of nearly sixty fiction and nonfiction books for children and adults. He received an undergraduate degree in communications from the Newhouse School at Syracuse University. This is Brett Friedman's second book.

Photo Credits

Cover, p.1 © Professor Oscar L. Miller/Science Photo Library; pp. 5, 8, 10, 11, 15, 16, 19, 27, 29, 30, 33 by Tahara Anderson; p. 13 © Professors P. Motta & T. Nagwo/Science Photo Library; p. 23 © Alfred Pasieka/Science Photo Library; p. 36 (left) © Stephen J. Krasemenn/Photo Researchers, Inc.; p. 36 (right) © Alexis Rosenfeld/Science Photo Library; p. 37 © Dr. Jeremy Burgess/Science Photo Library; p. 38 © Bettmann/Corbis.

Designer: Tahara Anderson; **Editor:** Joann Jovinelly